The Ghosts of You and Me

The Ghosts of You and Me

POEMS BY

Wesley McNair

For Patrick.

On the auspicious
occasion of your
first reading of a
magnificent poem:
"Reading the Signs".
With Thanks –

Wes McNair
5/9/09

DAVID R. GODINE · *Publisher*
BOSTON

First published in 2006 by
DAVID R. GODINE · *Publisher*
Post Office Box 450
Jaffrey, New Hampshire 03452
www.godine.com

LIBRARY OF CONGRESS
CATALOGING-IN-PUBLICATION DATA

McNair, Wesley.
The ghosts of you and me : poems / by Wesley McNair.
    p.   cm.
ISBN 1-56792-293-7
I. Title.
PS3563.C388G46 2006
811´.54—dc22
        2006006034

.

FIRST EDITION
Printed in the United States of America

for Diane

ACKNOWLEDGMENTS

Thanks to the following magazines in which poems of this
collection, sometimes in different form, have appeared:

Agni: "As Long As We Remember Him He Will Never Die,"
"If You Had Come," "The 1950s", "The End"; *Chautauqua Review*:
"As I Am"; *Connecticut Review*: "It," "To the Dog-Sitter"; *ForPoetry*:
"Stars," "The Gangsters of Old Movies"; *The Green Mountains Review*:
"Love Poem," "My Town"; *The Iowa Review*: "That Nothing," "The
Boy Carrying the Flag"; *MARGIE: A Review of American Poetry*:
"Hymn to the Comb-Over," "Imponderables," "Kuhre's Farm";
Mid-American Review: "Draw Me," "Flight," "The Sound the Dog
Made"; *New England Watershed*: "The Life," "The Man He Turned
Into." *Pleiades*: "Seeds," "The Side"; *The Sewanee Review*: "Mistakes
about Heaven," "My Mother Enters Heaven," "Ray's Gift," "The
Last Black and White TV," "Visiting Richard"; *Slate*: "As If the Voices
in the Background When My Mother Calls," "My Father Going
Away," "Questions at One O'Clock"; *The Southern Review*: "The
Future"; *The Faces of Americans in 1853*: "A Dream of Herman"; *The
Town of No*: "The Visit".

Thanks also to the Rockefeller Foundation for the 2005 fellowship
at the Bellagio Center which allowed the completion of this book.

Contents

The Boy Carrying the Flag

My Father Going Away

In a room far back in my mind
with strangers, my father
pressed the thick rim

of the glass to my mouth
burning my lips and throat,
then went back up

to where the laughter was.
My father was always
going away. "Where are you?"

I asked the tiny holes
in the phone my mother
handed me, unable to fit

his answer to my ear.
I spoke to my father
after he left us again

and again. Once, years
later, he was there,
wearing the odd, worn face

his real life had happened to,
and I, at the door of the present,
standing in the past. "I can't

hear you," I told him.
He was the slurred voice
that talked to itself

in a rental car while I
drove him through
the night to the city

where he would leave me
for the last time. Who were
the strangers who laughed

and drank with my father
in the house at the end
of the dark? All dead now,

and my father himself now dead,
but not before he twists
a twenty into my hand

next morning with his shaking
hand so hard I feel it
burning as I board the train.

Outside, my father going away
is waving and shouting
something that makes him

start toward me, something
he has held back all this time
behind the glass.

Flight

Like this, my mother said,
holding her arms out
from her sides
after my father left

as if she were flying,
then measured my arms
as I held them out
to fly. Soon I stood

by her sewing machine
trying to fly with white
patterns around my sleeves,
but missing my father

down where the feelings were.
Above me in her chair
she held the humming
light in her hands

tailoring sleeves
for the shirts
and suit coats that floated
in the half-dark

on hangers around her,
carried away by the spell
she made, safe from my father,
safe from me.

Straighten up! she pleaded
all through my childhood
as she ran her thumbs
over my wing bones

and pulled my shoulders
back. Up! Up!
And now my mother
cannot straighten,

though she denies it, bends
over even in her chair,
and when she walks
stooping down

where the love
and hardship are, she seems
to ask the earth
with each step why

it is taking hold
of her shoulders
and head this way – what
it could possibly want

with her. Or do I
alone ask these questions
she never taught me
as I grew up watching her,

wishing in spite of all
the evidence to fly.

Ray's Gift

When I saw him last, Norman
was an obese man with his own business
and two remote controls full of buttons
that brought in sports from around the world
while he sat high up in his Barcalounger
with a bag of chips in his lap – nothing like
the skinny kid my stepfather met
in the shop, who pushed the wheelbarrow
up the ramp from the cement mixer
to the forms for the foundation of our house
on weekends from morning till dark. How
my stepfather loved Norman's limitless appetite
for speed and work. Ray, with his bad heart,
stood and watched, smiling his shy
smile and shaking his head. "He
would never leave the shop like I'm
going to do," my stepfather told Norman
when Ray had gone back to his tumbledown
across the road. "He's just one of those types
that never catch on," he said, as if success
were a kind of static electricity he himself couldn't
help but cling to. Who would have thought
my stepfather would return to the machine shop
after his nursery business failed, and then,
having fired his help, would lie down
in the backyard all by himself to pull the transmission
down under the car, while it rolled off its blocks

and killed him? Barely two months before,
Norman died clutching his heart right
in his favorite chair. And there, standing beside
his wife when we opened the door
at my stepfather's wake, was Ray, she lifting
up a casserole, he smiling as he looked down,
half-embarrassed, holding nothing
but the flawed heart he had carried all
these years, and his gift of not catching on.

Draw Me

Inside the matchbook was the address
of the Famous Artists Correspondence School,
which was looking for talent, and on the front
was the illustration of a beautiful woman
above the words "Draw Me," as if drawing her

were a kind of lottery she was guessing
my stepfather, who held her in his hand
just four years before we met him,
would win. The woman he drew in the end
was my mother, with her three boys, and we

drew him, an odd fellow with a dangerous temper,
who could whistle like a bird with his throat,
and put us all to work building the house
and farm he dreamed of. The story he told
over and over of being chosen for the Famous

Artists School and working to save up
for the books they sent to him one by one
became our family story, and the classical head
in a bad drawing, all that remained
from his student lessons, was our family god,

displaying its chiseled surfaces behind glass
in our unfinished living room. For years,
while my mother cooked and sewed and my brothers
and I dug trenches for pipes and planted
evergreens that he claimed would pay for college

but grew in too close together, my stepfather worked
at the shop to pay for junk trucks and rototillers
he was determined to fix, and bigger
and bigger pumps to drive water uphill
from the river to his nursery, returning

each night to his chair beneath the faceted face
with the empty eyes to bow his head,
his desire sealed away by exhaustion,
god of working hard and saving up, god of will,
god of wishes, god of all the ways to draw stone.

Seeds

Dreaming of something else
held the three of them there
in the ghost room where it happened,

the man who had become
the father lifting the belt,
the only way he had ever

touched the boy, asking is this
what you wanted, the boy
saying no, no, dreaming

it would not hurt or last,
though it was just beginning,
the man with the belt caught

in the spell of his life-long
disappointment with what he wanted
and what he got, the boy's no

his no, and the mother, outside
the closed door of the room
dreaming too, her face shut

tight in the ecstasy
of the change that would now
surely come to that sad house,

as when the stepfather
finally opened the door
and left, it did come

to the boy, who knew it first
in his ears ringing with relief
in the silence of the room

where he lifted his pants
to carry the rounded
belt marks on his legs that hurt

and lasted until they transformed
into hard petals of brown on his skin,
and gradually turned to seeds.

Kuhre's Farm

Oh where is the oval mirror that held
each face above the washbasin
in the great kitchen, and where are the faces

of Rick, the hired man with no teeth
who drew the long, black comb
out of his overalls, proud of his hair,
and Andrew, the big, gentle son, who stooped
at the mirror and all the doorways

of that house, and his father, old Kuhre,
leaning on one crutch to watch himself
pass the washcloth slowly across the eyeless
right side of his face? And what
has happened to the room we entered then

to fold our hands before the covered
dishes and gravy boats of the last
dinners at noon in Cornish, New Hampshire,

while Kuhre's aged bride-by-mail
from the old country, who had left him
long ago for the risen Christ, spoke
words half in Danish for Him only,

and the old man seated at my left, stared
straight ahead with the eye he did not have,
eerily there and not there? Each day

on Kuhre's farm the cows walked slowly
out into the fields in their dream
of going out into the fields and each night
they dreamed of me waving my skinny arms

calling them back to the whitewashed
cobwebby barn, as I call them now,
latching them in their long rows of stalls
where they bawl for grain, and the tangled
barn cats cry for milk, and the milking machine
begins its great breathing and sighing

in the twilight. Here, inside that breathing,
is the window where I watch a black
Buick roll to a stop in the driveway

tipping its chrome teeth into the dust,
here is Les, the town man, slipping
once more through the door that leads
to the second floor and Andrew's wife

while Andrew sits and strokes the udders
of cows to strip them clean,

here are the three of them on the night
I'm asked upstairs, Les in his Hawaiian
shirt with Maggie on the couch, Andrew
by himself in overalls watching packs
of cigarettes with women's legs
dance in the blue light of the TV.

Oh on all my other nights I traveled
to another country, taking the washcloth
from its nail by the mirror above
the kitchen's basin as if taking a ticket

at the station window from my own ghost face,
and passing then to the dining room
with the lamp on the table to fold my hands
in the half-light beside the old woman
going away into the arms of Christ
and the stroke-bound man with one eye
gouged out by the horn of a cow. Yet

each day Kuhre went on walking step
by step, twisting himself between his crutches,
toward me as I pulled on the flywheel
of his ancient tractor until it began its chug-
chug-chug, shaking the ground, shaking
the raised cutter bar, shaking him
as he climbed slowly up its side and lay
his crutches carefully across the gear shift

and took the knob and held it fast, though it
shook in his knuckled hand. Kuhre held us all,

the old woman, the big son with the wife
who longed for the man from town,
and me, the boy raking the cut grass
while he circled me on his tractor, eye side

and eyeless side, though I hoped for rain,
and tuned my radio each night in my bed
until its lit eye opened and a voice
longing for love sang in the darkness.

Oh I am held still inside a silo in that place
of love promised and work going on,
treading and treading in the green rain
of silage that fell from a high window forever
before the time came

when Kuhre himself fell down, losing his hold
on the tractor with one quick stroke,

and Andrew's wife ran away
from the house with the covered dishes
and the oval mirror and the faces now gone,

and I, who dreamed of being free,
was set free from the silo, and from
the endless day after day in the lost fields
of Kuhre's farm, entering then my own life
of work and love and longing.

The Boy Carrying the Flag

Once, as the teenage boy marched up
and down the gutter with the wide blade
of a shovel above his head, and the goats
turned toward him in their stalls
undoing with their blats the band
music he held in his mind,

his stepfather, who had only asked,
for Christ's sake, to have the barn
cleaned out, rested his hand
on his hip in the doorway.
The boy would not have guessed
when he marched in his first parade

that he carried the flag for his stepfather,
or for his angry mother, also raised
for work and self-denial
during the Depression. Seeing him
dressed up like that to leave her stuck
on a failing farm with chores

as she had been stuck when she was just
his age, his mother remembered he forgot
to feed the chickens and refused
to drive him to the football game.
The old barns and dead cornfields
along the road in the sunless cold

had never seen a hitchhiker in red
wearing spats and lifting a white-
gloved thumb. Everyone stared
from the cars that passed him by,
and when at last he jumped down
from the door of a semi, the whole

marching band waiting in formation
by the buckling steps of the school
and Mr. Paskevitch, whose hands
twitched worse than ever, watched him
walk across the lawn looking
down at his size-fourteen black shoes.

Just one year from now, Paskevitch
would suffer a nervous breakdown
he would never return from,
but today, he raised the baton
to begin the only thing on earth
that could steady his hands, and the boy,

taller than the others, took his position
in the color guard, to carry the flag
for Paskevitch and for the sergeant-
at-arms, Pete LaRoche, so upset
by the hold-up he was screaming
his commands. For this first parade

belonged to LaRoche, too, and to O'Neill,
another son of immigrants, hoisting
the school colors, and to the rifle-bearers,
Wirkkala and Turco, the fat kid
who squinted helplessly against the wind.
Marching with a shuffle, Turco was already

resigned to his life in the shoe shop,
but this was before he went to work
on the night shift and drank all day,
and before Ann Riley, the head majorette
following the boy past the stopped
traffic kicking up her lovely legs,

got pregnant by the quarterback
and was forced to drop out
of the senior class. In this moment
of possibility in the unforgiving 1950s,
she wore nobody's ring around
her neck, and the boy imagined

how easily she had forgiven him
his lateness, and the times his mind
wandered and he fell out of step.
For in his secret heart he carried
the flag for Ann as he marched onto
the football field, leaving the town

with its three factories and wasted
farms far behind. There were LaRoche's
and O'Neill's mothers, on their day off
from the flock mill, and there
were the fathers in their shop pants,
and the classmates in school jackets,

and the teachers who looked strange
without their ties, all applauding
and shouting while the band, capped,
plumed, and lifting up the shining bells
of their instruments, marched by –
all here on this dark and windy day

to watch the quarterback, Joe Costello,
Ann's lover-to-be, lead them into the sun,
as were the band and the tallest boy
in the color guard himself,
carrying the stars and stripes
for everyone who was here

and not here in this broken town,
and for their hope in the uncertain
promise that struggled
against his hand as he marched
to his place on the bleachers
among these, his fellow Americans.

The Last Black and White TV

It

Don't fall for it.
Don't scratch it.
Don't spoil it for everyone else.
Don't take it for granted.

It's not anything to play with.
It's not the end of the world.
It's not brain surgery.
That's not it.

I used to have cravings for it.
It's the last thing I need right now.
I wish it would just go away.
I can't take it anymore.

Why is it so important to you?
Why did you laugh about it?
Why can't you just be quiet about it?
Is it all about you?

It's all sticky.
It's giving me the creeps.
It's worse than I thought.
You're getting it all over yourself.

This is no place for it.
There's no excuse for it.
Take it outside.
Get over it.

Imponderables

1

Does anybody live
in the trailer on the way
to the dump with the chimney
and the washed-out American
flag hanging from the antenna,
and if so, which car
outside is the one
that runs?

2

Who decided it would look nice
to have the four pines
growing so close together
beside the road, they'd have no
branches except what sprouted
twenty feet above the broken-
spine farmhouse like
palm fronds?

3

What happened to the customer
who ordered the gray stack
of long boards and the gray
stack of short boards

growing vetch and morning glories
by the billboard advertising Dan's
Custom Sawing, and what
happened to Dan?

4

When will they sell
their peeling, curtainless place
at the top of the sidehill pasture,
now that they've moved across
the road to the brand-new double-wide
next to the cow barn, leaving
behind the sign that says For Sale,
House Only?

The Sound the Dog Made

After the old man died
leaving Doris, the younger woman
who co-owned the trailer park
and reminded him of his dead wife,
the only phone number she would need

to pay for his final arrangements,
and after she called that number
to find it had been disconnected,
and the second younger woman,
not so young now, turned up

in the driveway, waving a will
that resembled the will
her husband, Larry, the trailer park's
other owner, had kept safe
behind the microwave, and after

the third younger woman, the oldest,
called her from the home,
referring to the signed document
that her son-in-law, taking the phone,
said was also notarized,

Doris was in no mood to think
about the dog, the last of four
dachshunds, each named "Snoopy"
by the old man, after his wife's dog
from long before, so on the night

when he ripped out his tube and returned
to his trailer from the hospital,
it seemed they were one continuous
dog he had come home to see,
sitting down with his ruined kidneys

on the bed and turning back
the covers to pat the sheet with the same
soft gesture he had used for all
the Snoopys of thirty-five years,
which was part of the reason

the dog, now an old man himself,
let go of his bowels and would not stop
with his racket until Larry
opened the door the next morning
and found the old man lying in the bed

he would have to be lifted from
and that crazy, god-damn dog
wandering lost in his own filth,
as Larry put it in his report
to his wife, the last of the continuous

younger women, who had just wanted
what she had been promised, after all,
so Doris ended up disgusted
with both the dog and the old man
she had spent all her time

taking care of only to discover
he had nothing to his name,
signed or otherwise, but his trailer
and a junk car still unpaid for,
and she couldn't understand,

for the life of her, why,
after they had finally got the dog
put down and the old man taken out
of the park, Larry had to keep
going on about the sound the dog made

that morning in the trailer, high-pitched,
he said, but not a howl exactly, and not
really barking either, at least not the kind
dogs do when they're begging
for somebody to give them a biscuit.

To the Dog-Sitter

Once she flings her old self
down on the rug, she'll look
so much like a frayed
rag, you'll be amazed
to see her recompose
into head and legs and walk
from room to room,
unable to recall whether
she's hungry or needs to pee.
Right then, let her out,
but remember that her nose,
alert to meanings in the slightest
breeze, is still the prophet
the rest of her, half-blind, lame
and lost, will follow anywhere.

Hymn to the Comb-Over

How the thickest of them erupt just
above the ear, cresting in waves so stiff
no wind can move them. Let us praise them
in all of their varieties, some skinny
as the bands of headphones, some rising
from a part that extends halfway around
the head, others four or five strings
stretched so taut the scalp resembles
a musical instrument. Let us praise the sprays
that hold them, and the combs that coax
such abundance to the front of the head
in the mirror, the combers entirely forget
the back. And let us celebrate the combers,
who address the old sorrow of time's passing
day after day, bringing out of the barrenness
of mid-life this ridiculous and wonderful
harvest, no wishful flag of hope, but, thick,
or thin, the flag itself, unfurled for us all
in subways, offices, and malls across America.

The End

How quaint lovemaking was in the old
movies, the lovers saving it for the end
which was called The End, and all
dressed up for it, though everybody knows

the whole idea is to take your clothes off
as they do in films today, undoing each other
button by belt buckle because they can't
wait to start their love scene,

which is the old one upside-down,
not a grand finale of faces confessing
to each other, but interlocking legs
and thighs leading to the faces

of the waitress and the guy she met at the end
of the night shift, grimacing and panting.
Life is simply like that, the next day
comes through the curtains and he discovers

she has a kid who doesn't like him,
or she can't look him in the eye
because he wasn't able to perform
and the shrink, who made him recount

all this, looks up from his notebook
in the sudden quiet of his office
with professional curiosity. Not us,
we understand he was trying too hard

to forget the lover he broke up with,
or perhaps he was using this one-night-stand
to escape the threat of her career,
or maybe the shrink is talking to a woman

who turns out to be the daughter
of the waitress, in trouble with men
because she had no father and her mother
slept around. Poor kid, in a woman's body,

which we are bound to see every
part of as she searches for fulfillment
on her own dark island of shifting legs
and thighs: it's not easy to find love

today, when there's too little of it
or too much with the wrong person.
But just for tonight, my love,
let's break out the popcorn and bring back

the old hero, who pushes the hair
away from the face of his lover
as he holds her, lost in that sky.
Let's pretend with them that love is not

an island, but a wide shore at the end
of all life's sorrows, where lovers
can meet at last to live on nothing
but the light in each other's eyes.

The Gangsters of Old Movies

The cars they stole looked as square
as the small-town chumps
who owned them, like a kind of house
with a step in front of the door

and two rooms inside that had couches
and vases for flowers between
the windows. Automobiles,
they were called, the name

of what it felt like for some sap
and his family to sit still
while their overstuffed seats
moved down the street

as if by themselves. Floor it,
said the gangsters of old movies,
squealing their tires, which had nothing
to do with pretty flowers or going

to grandmother's house. So what
if the thug on the running board
with the heater fell off right in front
of the cops, they were on their way

to the hideout to split the take.
The gangsters of old movies
were in love with motion,
which was why, among the others

who saved their cars in garages
for Sunday drives, they never fit in,
and why, when they entered the bank
to find the place as still

as a lending library or a museum
where all the dough was kept
behind glass, they felt like
shooting holes in the ceiling

and getting the tellers and the bank
president out from behind the bars
to roll around in the lobby and beg
for their lives. How could they explain

to these hopeless throwbacks
to another century that life
was about the pleasures of money
and screwing people out of it

with the engine running,
not quite knowing they belonged
in another century themselves?
Never mind that the little thug

who was always nervous
about making it to the big time
finally sings like a canary to put them
behind bars, too, and forget

the canned lecture on upholding the law
in the last reel that sounds
like a civics lesson by an old maid
in a one-room school,

and rewind to the getaway scene
of the largest heist in history,
where the Boss, in a back seat
with the life savings of all the pigeons

in the heartland tucked away
in his suitcase, sits as unfazed
as a CEO off for the holidays.
See how, in the perfect meeting

of speed and greed, their black cars
hit the main street among sirens
with the authority of a presidential
motorcade. Look again

at how easily they ditch the cops
and turn their square automobiles
into spirals of dust, on the road
to the Future of Our Country.

The 1950s

"Let's take the car after school," the two girls
would say, which meant they wanted to be taken
by it, the top down, the wind surfing over
the wrap-around window. The stepdaughter,

Carol, always drove, just as her new stepfather
insisted, and while her girlfriend Debbie listened
for the lighter to pop out from the dash
and with its tiny, interior hotplate lit menthol

cigarettes one by one for both of them, they thought
about how the boys would admire them.
When they drove into their station at the A&W
and Carol unhooked the mike to order their Cokes

pushing back her shoulder-length hair to reveal
her long throat, she thought she resembled
a popular singer. "Beautiful" was the word
the boys used to describe the car as they gathered

around it, stroking its curves and sometimes
asking if they could see what was under
the hood. Then they looked into Carol's amazing
and frightening blue eyes, or Debbie's warm,

compliant ones, the door or fender giving them a way
to steady themselves. All of that was OK
with the stepfather, who required only that they let
no boys inside, or they could never borrow

the car again. Handsome like a man, he really wasn't
much more than a boy himself, and not wanting to be
anyone's father, told them to call him "Petey."
As he said goodbye in his T-shirt some afternoons,

leaning comfortably into the open window of his new
Chevy convertible, he would call Debbie
"Ginger Snap," and his stepdaughter, his favorite,
with a knowing wink, "Angel Pie." He was proud

of the sinuous Hawaiian woman in green he wore
on his muscular forearm and the darker tattoo
in cursive letters of his own name underneath, the same
tattoo he had his new wife ink on the inside

of her ankle. "Don't you go changing on me,"
he would say with a smile before they headed out
the driveway and the motion rose in their ears, but
the two in the car were already changing, Debbie,

who hoped each day at the A&W for a certain
cute boy to return her gaze, and Carol, in distress
because she couldn't quite get the muscular forearm
and the wink out of her mind even after she touched

her cigarette to the lighter and took a deep
drag and tried to find a good station on the radio.

Questions at One O'Clock

On the religious program the visiting pastor
is roasting the host behind the desk
about how much weight he put on.
The host comes right back about
the pastor's hairline. Are they trying
to show that God enjoys a good joke, like us?
When the mood changes and the camera
moves closer to the host's pressed
eyelids, does he believe his promise
that we will know the meaning of Christ's
sacrifice if we send him the pledge
he requests of us? There is nobody to ask.
It is one o'clock in the morning, and the streets
are rainy and dark outside the TV store
where ten hosts are praying all at once
in different flesh tones. A woman pushing
a shopping cart walks by wearing their faces
and the repeated red color of the host's tie
on her back. Passing cars flash streaks
of flesh and red from their closed windows.

The Last Black and White TV

Were your parents, or you yourself
among those children who left their primitive
games of giant steps and hopscotch to gather
like stunned pygmies before cowboys
and puppets moving in the light of the first

black and white TVs, square bulbs so heavy
it took two men to deliver them? As night
came on in suburban neighborhoods
perhaps like yours, families unfolded
the legs of dinner trays, longing

to be in the studio audience with the host
of the variety show, or in the white kitchen
with the mother and her children as the father
arrived at the right moment in his dark suit
with the knowledge the rest of them craved.

"It needs more contrast," someone would say,
adjusting a knob until the vegetable slicer
they saw between programs or the black and white
shoes or the kitchen range with the glow-clock
in the changing world behind the glass

looked real, then bought the slicer, the shoes,
the kitchen range, and even the new TV
that their old TV said would make them feel
like they were there. This was how the first
black and white TVs made their way

to the homes of the poor, who loved them best,
turning from disappointment all day long
to watch people opening the doors of ranges
and cars, or men with easy-going smiles
give them away on game shows. When they kicked

their sets or pounded them, it was mostly
because the picture was starting to roll
and ruin the happy ending they were so anxious
to see. The last black and white TV might have been
one of these, its console scarred by fists,

flipping scenes of game show contestants
and sheriffs bringing justice to Americans long ago
in the West up out of sight again and again.
Or it may have been the set that played itself to death
above the heads of old folks at the nursing home

in the suburbs, grown sick of wonder and desire.
Or perhaps it stares by the old color set into the dust
of your own attic among things you once discovered
on the screen and would hardly imagine longing for,
they are so strange, so useless, and so still.

As Long As We Remember Him

Visiting Richard

When Richard, just
one year ago a poet
and scholar, lifts his eyes
from his comic book

to look at you, you can't
see inside him. He is all
outside now, wearing
spectacles someone else

tucked behind his ears
to balance on his nose,
and a shirt whose one
unfastened button

somebody else forgot.
Yet see as he bends
his head how tenderly
his thumb and forefinger

take the corner of each
page, turning it over
to the fingers that smooth it
under his absent eyes.

See how Richard's hands
remember what he loved.

The Side

The side that dragged its foot
and swung its hand
and waited for the thump
of the cane over and over.

The side that had to be led around by the hand
of her other side.

The side that was always hanging around.

The side her other side learned to put into
the hole of a sleeve.

The side her other side
put lipstick on, unfolding
the lips with the tube.

The side that wouldn't lift
a muscle to help.

The side that was retired.

The side of her mouth that chewed without feeling
the food collecting outside
itself.

The side the living eye lived in
under a dead lid.

The side that when they bathed
and toweled it
did not seem to her
to be her.

The side that came
to be her.

If You Had Come

If you had come into that room
after her stroke to find
my mother-in-law Sue Reed
and me, our heads bent
toward each other, making faces

so her face would remember
what it had forgot
of the expressions for surprise
and dismay, or if
you had come in the moment

I tried to teach her lips
by forming small lips
and making them breathe,
first to the left, then
to the right of my nose

until she began to laugh,
and laugh because she couldn't
on one side, and both
of us laughed, you might
have imagined what we did

had less to do with instruction
or sorrow than the antics
of lovers, she giving me
her hand then, I taking it
in mine to stroke it

over and over in the pleasure
of being together in the room
where you might have come
to imagine the two of us
together, just as we were.

As Long As We Remember Him
He Will Never Die

they said, which explained
why he ended up beside his wife
at the funeral home, not a presence
with a suit and wristwatch,

but a kind of feeling she had.
Others had it too,
so in the days after the funeral,
he would find himself

going down the thruway
in the back seat with his co-workers
from the car pool, or driving
out of the parking lot

at the supermarket, where
days after he was in the ground,
his neighbor swore she saw him.
Getting behind the wheel again

or sitting at breakfast
with his daughter as she recalled
how many sugars he used
in his coffee seemed

too good to be true, because
it wasn't exactly, he being absent
as the space on the bed
his wife reached for,

drawing him to her in this way
that made him immaterial.
Besides, he wasn't there
any longer than it took them

to return to the relentless
motion and change they lived for.
So after he came back
and discovered the counselor

handing his wife a box of tissues
while urging her to put
the past behind her
and move on, and after

he hovered in frustration
above the grandson who tried
to recall him from
the photograph in the album,

and after hearing the conversation
of a man asking whatever happened
to him, and another man
answering, "He's dead,"

he was ready to die
his second death, as he did,
released piece by piece
from each memory until at last

he was gone to that place
where, like them, you and I also
would have been afraid
all that time to lose him,

beyond motion and recalling
and forgetting.

Mistakes About Heaven

I

Contrary to what is said,
longing exists there.
Imagine the soul as one
so involved with the music
as it played the game
of walking around the chairs,
it discovered too late
that it had no chair. Having lived
its only life in the body,
it sometimes misses
the walking and the sitting down
and above all, the music.

2

Having done bad things
can actually get you in,
particularly if you have been
a parent, and did bad things
for the love of your children.

3

Swearing is perfectly okay there,
even though it's hardly practiced,
cursing being a response

to frustrations on earth
that stand in the way
of mortal service. These God damns
every time He is asked.

4

The ones who deny themselves
all enjoyment in preparation
for heaven gain admission
only because God
feels sorry for them.
There is pleasure in heaven.
God is known
for the way He parties.

5

Since the basest
of human motivations
are storing up wealth
beyond measure
and plotting for one's own
future, as the sermon
recommends, they have no
honor in heaven.

6

The holiest are not the men
who once looked upward
in front of others
in suits or robes
to speak to a ghost,
but the forgotten ones
who sat beside trash barrels
or beneath an overpass
listening to voices,
unsure of which to follow.
Heaven is not up
or down but a place outside
programs. Those most
ready for it have spent
their lives unable
to make up their minds.

7

Mysteries are not solved.
The most heavenly experience
is the feeling, as in art,
of something imminent
that never quite

takes place. This is the feeling
those who go there
inhabit always.

As If the Voices in the Background When My Mother Calls

late at night have just started
partying.

As if when she calls in the morning
they have stayed up
to be with her
all night.

As if what I say makes them erupt
into laughter and applause.

As if when she uses
the first name of the news anchor
he is someone we both know.

As if they sit with her
in chairs not already
occupied with newspapers. As if

they hadn't noticed the pathways
through her living room
are only wide enough
for one.

As if in the moment
before she hung up
forgetting to leave a message
the voices

left their own message.
As if when she

is no longer there they
will go on
without her.

My Mother Enters Heaven

She is pleased they had the sense
to choose her, and arriving here at last
beside her husband, the one she's spent
the final years of her life proving wrong,

is just what she dreamed of for herself
those long afternoons working in the nursery
he cursed for all the money it lost. "I spent
all my time propagating that forsythia

you discovered, and even got it into
a catalogue," she tells him, speaking the words
she imagined each time she lifted
the spout of her watering can to her pots

inside the tumbledown plastic hut,
her unsold shrubs tangled across the paths
outside. So why does Paul just stand there
balancing that thin, sparking aureole

above his head and gone away in his eye
as if he is alive somewhere, just not here?
If she were back on earth in the spring
she was just taken from, she would pluck off

a twig bearing the delicate yellow flower
and place it in his hand to take away
that expression of longsuffering
and make him pay attention to how good

she has been and how well everything
turned out, even though she had to sell off
the two main growing fields. But Paul's hand,
which she hasn't touched since years before

the junk car he lay down underneath
to undo the transmission rolled off
its blocks and killed him – the hand
just dangles there all creepy and dead

to her. It is so quiet here, she begins
to think all over again about the fight
they had, their worst, on the evening
she found him, how Paul kicked the dirt

in the greenhouse and cursed it, then
cursed her for binding him to it,
and afterward how quiet it was around her
in that place, too, until at last she walked

out by the barn to the source of the silence,
which was the dropped car, and beneath it
his upturned hand, open in welcome
as if to taunt her. All she wanted then

was to flee the hand, but now, standing
in the light of all things made clear,
she holds it and rubs it, wanting only for Paul
to come back free of this halo and the peace

beyond human understanding and understand.
It is in this moment the sparking begins to form
above her own face shining with tears,
and his hand in hers, my mother enters heaven.

The Ghosts of You and Me

The Future

Married that young, with three children
and one more on the way, I lived far
from the still, beautiful place
where writers and scholars were photographed
in the early 1960s, so I studied each detail of it
on their dust jackets – the neat spines
of books arranged around them as they sat
contemplating something at the edge
of the picture frame in their sweaters
or tweeds, pipes in their hands. Buying a pipe
to hold in my hand, too, I couldn't quite
get over the taste of tar, and when I puffed it
in the calm, unhurried way I imagined,
it always went out. Which was why
I tapped it that day on the wastebasket
behind me, not exactly in a university office,
but in my home room at the high school,
where I sat contemplating the conundrum
of Brenda and Brian who had asked
what was going to happen to their dreams
for the future, now that she was pregnant.
They, so intent on my answer,
I trying one more time to puff
on my pipe, nobody saw the light
behind us at first, then my two students,
who had thought it was cool to have
a teacher who helped solve their problems

and lit his pipe up right in school, began
to shout at me until I turned, and we all
watched the wastebasket seem to lift up
with the flames that rose to the blackboard,
then fell to sparks floating among random
wisps of gray, and just like that were gone.

Stars

After the one more day
of work that leaves his work
undone, he wakes

deep in winter in the farmhouse
on the curve of the road,
his dear companion

and children held fast
by the silence that seems
to him like death, and listens

to the muffled if,
if, if of a downshifting truck
rounding the corner to discover

in snow and ice the nearly
impossible hill, then listens
to the car after car

traveling down, so intent
on how they slow
at the unpredicted, dangerous

turn just below him groping
in their cave of light,
no one could show him

what he sees in the corner
of his eye, these strange, beautiful
flashes moving by reflection

across the sky of his room,
each opening a window
quickly out of a window to make

its long, bright point, the stars
he has saved in spite of himself
all these years from the dark.

The Man He Turned Into

All he wanted was companionship
for his journey and a chair to sit in
while he held his pen and gazed
at his shape-shifting friends,
the clouds, so how has he ended up

with a wife and four children
driving down the highway, his gas
almost gone, holding a steering wheel
that shakes in his hands? What's out
of balance is not only the front end

of his car, but the ratio of his bills
to the pay he gets for teaching English
in high school and, during summers,
mixing milkshakes, house paint,
or cement, which is why,

rather than clouds, he is gazing
at the warning level on his fuel gauge,
hoping this car with bad alignment
and the great harelip the accident
has made in the chrome mouth

of its grille will get him home.
He is, after all, just four miles away
now that he's stopped at the post office
for the mail, done with a day he only
wants to forget, and would have forgotten

except for the envelope that sticks out
from among the bills and second bills
on the passenger seat, returned
from the editor he sent his poem to.
It will only cause disruption if he opens it

to find his poem hasn't been accepted,
and even if the poem has, he could
turn into a twenty-eight year old man
with trembling hands who screams
and weeps above the whine

of scalloped tires that in his broken-
down life he has found a form at last,
the very man he finally does turn into
when he opens it.

A Dream of Herman

for Diane

I was driving the old Dodge wagon
again, with Coke cans rolling to the front
at stop signs, and you rubbing the dash
every so often to thank the car
for not needing the spare tire
we hadn't fixed. We were on a trip
that felt like going to your father's camp,
only we never got there, and didn't care.
It was a beautiful day, just enough wind
coming into the back to make the kids
squint with pure pleasure as it
scribbled their hair, and your mother
patted them, saying what a nice ride it was
in the odd, small voice she used only
for your father. It was then in the rearview
mirror I saw him, wearing the brown
cardigan he always wore and putting on
the radiant bell of his saxophone as if
just back from an intermission.
You were smiling, and suddenly
I saw the reason we were traveling together
and did not want to stop was Herman,
who just sat there in the cargo space
breathing the scale until the whole family
sat back in their seats, and then he lifted
his sax and opened one more song as wide
and delicate as the floating trees.

The Visit

We were at the camp, it must have been
some afternoon that summer
after your Aunt Ruth's stroke
because her mouth looked skeptical,
almost provocative, as if she had suddenly
achieved the role of the great lady
she'd spent a lifetime preparing for.
And I remember how, with this new
dignity, she turned to Uncle Herb's thought
about how good a beer would taste as if
he weren't wearing Bermuda shorts
and wing-tipped shoes at all,
but a loincloth. How could he
have known she would relent in just
a few minutes and, what was more,
(the porch had got so hot, even with
the breeze) Aunt Ruth would feel
compelled to have one too? So
what Herb came back with was beers
for everybody, even Ruth's 80-
year-old sister, do you remember,
the one who was shrinking and said Oh,
because she liked the cheese
your mother brought out or the small flowers
on the TV tray or the wind that threatened
to blow her wide hat off? It didn't,
of course, and when Ruth said No, no, no,

Herbert, we knew he could go on telling
what they did when they were younger,
because it had turned out to be
one of those wonderful days that had nothing
quite to do with wind or words. So Herb
just sat there, his white legs happy
to be free of dress pants, and talked – was it
about the wildest party, or how fast they drove
in his new car afterward? And though
they said they couldn't stay, they stayed
until the last light rose into the tops
of the trees around us on the pond,
and the wind suddenly stopped,
and even Aunt Ruth said how nice
it had got. Perfection
is what almost doesn't happen.

The Life

The birches come down
to the water's edge
to look at the image

of themselves,
and above them the clouds
gather amazed at how deep

they are, though nothing
in this unsubstantial
place is ever there

for long. Over and over
the shadows of docks
and boats

floating upside-down
are suddenly undone,
and the great

pondside stones are shaken
to bits and carried
away. Yet see

how the clouds return,
and on the point
through seams of light

the firs and pines
are opening limb by limb.
See how they grow

straight down
again, trembling
in their second life.

That Nothing

In the moment
of your giving up,
the lost keys suddenly
meeting your eyes
from the only place
you could have put them.

The forgotten table
and open book and empty
chair waiting for you
all this time
in the light left on.

A shade lifted
by your loved one
waking upstairs,
the sound
you did not know
you listened for.

The mysterious
penmanship of snow
the branches of a tree
have brought you,
standing at your own door.

Nothing ever happens here.
That nothing.

As I Am

Behind my false beard
and the frown line between
the eyebrows I have developed

by trying to pay attention
to the world, I am the same kid
who could never remember

his library books or what
he had been sent to the store for.
"Fog" was the name my teachers

gave to where I spent my time,
a haze that even today
can descend while I'm having

a conversation, or suddenly lift,
revealing the wrong
landmarks drifting past me

on the wrong road I took ten
miles ago. God, it has been lonely
to turn up all those years

where everyone else has arrived
long since. Yet how, without
looking just beyond

the shoulders of others
as they spoke, or searching
everywhere for the pen

I found in my own hand,
could I concentrate on the thought
I learned to write down

at last, back from the place
that has wanted me off-course
and bewildered, just as I am.

My Town

Where it belongs on the state
tourist map, well above the red lobster
on the coast and in between the man
skiing down the slope and the shining dome
of the capitol building, you'll find nothing
except a moose standing in the grass.
But who would come to this place

to see the three-foot long spotted
yellow butterflies faithfully displayed
on the side of LaFlamme's house, or gather
with the others in the Grange Hall to hear
Ethel Chadwick recite with a lisp
and the dazed, oddly beautiful look
in her eye "The Cremation of Sam McGee"

in its entirety on Old Home Day?
Anyway, what (as people from the city
might say after straying off Route 2
to find our few houses thrown downhill
among the trees) do they do here
for work? Nothing important, as you might
guess from how early in the morning

they start up the hill to do it, driving
to the shoe shop two towns over,
or the paper mill, or just down the road

to the store, where Betty DeCarlo stands all
day at the counter asking the same question:
"Can I help you?" I'm the one waiting
in line behind the couple with the skis

on their minivan who don't even notice her alert,
genuine eyes, on their way through Eyeblink,
Maine, to someplace they've heard of,
and I'm the one lying awake listening
to the cars struggling up our hill in the darkness
of five A.M. to start their long day,
and at twilight sitting down in the old parlor

with the Redlevskis, that's me, with a bag
of rhubarb I've just picked from my garden
for the two of them. On the television
in the corner a frowning man, on mute,
mimes all the news of concern to the nation.
Meanwhile, they are talking about how good
it is to eat fresh sticks of rhubarb raw, a concern

so small you wouldn't care much about it
unless you could be there to see the face
she makes for the taste, a mixture of sorrow
and pleasure that seems to have her whole life
in it, and to hear, in the lamplight, the intimate
twang of their voices telling me this news
at evening in my town, as I'm telling it

to you now, in this only other place I know
where unexpected things can happen, off the map.

Love Poem

In the beautiful double light of the pond,
our day together has seemed more
than a single day, and now the sunset
clouds of the pond's second sky stretch
all the way from our dock chairs

to Lucy Point, which had no name
until Lucy, Bob and Rita's dog, began
swimming ahead of them to reach it.
Imagine that the pond, which gradually
deepens the red of our sky, remembers

another sky, where the three of them
swim together for the first time,
unaware of the likeness beneath them.
Imagine this is the pond taking them in
with the wide, unblinking eye of its

perpetual knowing and remembering,
where all the days are one day. Here
is the loon that left behind the small, white
after-image of its breast, here above a brown
shadow is the beaver slowly moving

its nose-print. Around it is a darkening
twilight like ours, decades ago, when
the ghost of Harland Hutchinson,
on the roof of the pond's original camp,
brings his hammer down in silence

making the delayed echo of each blow,
which is the pond listening and storing
the sound away in its pond mind. There,
my love, if you can imagine, it is always
twilight, and always the morning after

the hard freeze, when long-dead Caroline
Barlach, up from New York City to winter
in her godforsaken shack and write the great
American novel, bends toward the hole
she has cut in the ice for water to create,

unknown to her, a shaggy, unforgettable
cameo of her face. For nothing in the quick
double-knowing of the pond is ever lost,
though on this night as the wind comes up,
the single cry of a loon falls away

somewhere beyond Lucy Point,
and the reflection of the pines that rim
the pond darkens around us, and the ghosts
of you and me, barely visible off our dock,
break apart on waves beside a shifting moon.

Wesley McNair's volumes of poetry include six collections and two limited editions. He has also published books of essays and three anthologies of Maine writing. A recipient of Fulbright and Guggenheim fellowships, he has received two NEA grants, and has twice been awarded Rockefeller fellowships for creative work at the Bellagio Center on Lake Como in Italy. His honors in poetry include the Theodore Roethke Prize, the Eunice Tietjens Prize, the Jane Kenyon Award, and the Sarah Josepha Hale Medal. He lives with his wife Diane in Mercer, Maine.

DESIGN & COMPOSITION BY CARL W. SCARBROUGH